THIS BOOK BELONGS TO:

_____

Change your PASSWORD to "incorrect". Everytime you forget it, it will remind you: "Your password is incorrect".

PASSWORD TRACKER

| SOC MEDIA | PERSONAL | WORK | GAMES | SHOPPING |

WEBSITE

USERNAME

LOG IN/USER ID

PASSWORD

EMAIL LINKED

CONTACT # LINKED

SECURITY QUESTION

SECURITY ANSWER

NOTES

_____
_____
_____
_____
_____
_____
_____
_____
_____
_____

PASSWORD TRACKER

| SOC MEDIA | PERSONAL | WORK | GAMES | SHOPPING |

WEBSITE

USERNAME

LOG IN/USER ID

PASSWORD

EMAIL LINKED

CONTACT # LINKED

SECURITY QUESTION

SECURITY ANSWER

NOTES

_____
_____
_____
_____
_____
_____
_____
_____
_____
_____

PASSWORD TRACKER

| ☐ SOC MEDIA | ☐ PERSONAL | ☐ WORK | ☐ GAMES | ☐ SHOPPING |

WEBSITE

USERNAME

LOG IN/USER ID

PASSWORD

EMAIL LINKED

CONTACT # LINKED

SECURITY QUESTION

SECURITY ANSWER

NOTES

_____
_____
_____
_____
_____
_____
_____
_____
_____
_____

PASSWORD TRACKER

| SOC MEDIA | PERSONAL | WORK | GAMES | SHOPPING |

- WEBSITE
- USERNAME
- LOG IN/USER ID
- PASSWORD
- EMAIL LINKED
- CONTACT # LINKED
- SECURITY QUESTION
- SECURITY ANSWER

NOTES

_____
_____
_____
_____
_____
_____
_____
_____
_____

PASSWORD TRACKER

| SOC MEDIA | PERSONAL | WORK | GAMES | SHOPPING |

- **WEBSITE**
- **USERNAME**
- **LOG IN/USER ID**
- **PASSWORD**
- **EMAIL LINKED**
- **CONTACT # LINKED**
- **SECURITY QUESTION**
- **SECURITY ANSWER**

NOTES

_____
_____
_____
_____
_____
_____
_____
_____
_____

PASSWORD TRACKER

| SOC MEDIA | PERSONAL | WORK | GAMES | SHOPPING |

- WEBSITE
- USERNAME
- LOG IN/USER ID
- PASSWORD
- EMAIL LINKED
- CONTACT # LINKED
- SECURITY QUESTION
- SECURITY ANSWER

NOTES

_____
_____
_____
_____
_____
_____
_____
_____
_____

PASSWORD TRACKER

| SOC MEDIA | PERSONAL | WORK | GAMES | SHOPPING |

WEBSITE

USERNAME

LOG IN/USER ID

PASSWORD

EMAIL LINKED

CONTACT # LINKED

SECURITY QUESTION

SECURITY ANSWER

NOTES

_____
_____
_____
_____
_____
_____
_____
_____
_____

PASSWORD TRACKER

| SOC MEDIA | PERSONAL | WORK | GAMES | SHOPPING |

- **WEBSITE**
- **USERNAME**
- **LOG IN/USER ID**
- **PASSWORD**
- **EMAIL LINKED**
- **CONTACT # LINKED**
- **SECURITY QUESTION**
- **SECURITY ANSWER**

NOTES

_____
_____
_____
_____
_____
_____
_____
_____
_____
_____

PASSWORD TRACKER

| SOC MEDIA | PERSONAL | WORK | GAMES | SHOPPING |

- WEBSITE
- USERNAME
- LOG IN/USER ID
- PASSWORD
- EMAIL LINKED
- CONTACT # LINKED
- SECURITY QUESTION
- SECURITY ANSWER

NOTES

_____
_____
_____
_____
_____
_____
_____
_____
_____

PASSWORD TRACKER

| SOC MEDIA | PERSONAL | WORK | GAMES | SHOPPING |

- WEBSITE
- USERNAME
- LOG IN/USER ID
- PASSWORD
- EMAIL LINKED
- CONTACT # LINKED
- SECURITY QUESTION
- SECURITY ANSWER

NOTES

_____
_____
_____
_____
_____
_____
_____
_____
_____
_____

PASSWORD TRACKER

| SOC MEDIA | PERSONAL | WORK | GAMES | SHOPPING |

WEBSITE

USERNAME

LOG IN/USER ID

PASSWORD

EMAIL LINKED

CONTACT # LINKED

SECURITY QUESTION

SECURITY ANSWER

NOTES

_____
_____
_____
_____
_____
_____
_____
_____
_____

PASSWORD TRACKER

| SOC MEDIA | PERSONAL | WORK | GAMES | SHOPPING |

WEBSITE

USERNAME

LOG IN/USER ID

PASSWORD

EMAIL LINKED

CONTACT # LINKED

SECURITY QUESTION

SECURITY ANSWER

NOTES

_____
_____
_____
_____
_____
_____
_____
_____
_____

PASSWORD TRACKER

☐ SOC MEDIA ☐ PERSONAL ☐ WORK ☐ GAMES ☐ SHOPPING

WEBSITE

USERNAME

LOG IN/USER ID

PASSWORD

EMAIL LINKED

CONTACT # LINKED

SECURITY QUESTION

SECURITY ANSWER

NOTES

PASSWORD TRACKER

| SOC MEDIA | PERSONAL | WORK | GAMES | SHOPPING |

- WEBSITE
- USERNAME
- LOG IN/USER ID
- PASSWORD
- EMAIL LINKED
- CONTACT # LINKED
- SECURITY QUESTION
- SECURITY ANSWER

NOTES
_____
_____
_____
_____
_____
_____
_____
_____
_____

PASSWORD TRACKER

| SOC MEDIA | PERSONAL | WORK | GAMES | SHOPPING |

WEBSITE

USERNAME

LOG IN/USER ID

PASSWORD

EMAIL LINKED

CONTACT # LINKED

SECURITY QUESTION

SECURITY ANSWER

NOTES

PASSWORD TRACKER

| ☐ SOC MEDIA | ☐ PERSONAL | ☐ WORK | ☐ GAMES | ☐ SHOPPING |

- **WEBSITE** _____
- **USERNAME** _____
- **LOG IN/USER ID** _____
- **PASSWORD** _____
- **EMAIL LINKED** _____
- **CONTACT # LINKED** _____
- **SECURITY QUESTION** _____
- **SECURITY ANSWER** _____

NOTES

_____
_____
_____
_____
_____
_____
_____
_____

PASSWORD TRACKER

| | SOC MEDIA | | PERSONAL | | WORK | | GAMES | | SHOPPING |

- **WEBSITE**
- **USERNAME**
- **LOG IN/USER ID**
- **PASSWORD**
- **EMAIL LINKED**
- **CONTACT # LINKED**
- **SECURITY QUESTION**
- **SECURITY ANSWER**

NOTES

_____
_____
_____
_____
_____
_____
_____
_____
_____

PASSWORD TRACKER

| SOC MEDIA | PERSONAL | WORK | GAMES | SHOPPING |

- WEBSITE
- USERNAME
- LOG IN/USER ID
- PASSWORD
- EMAIL LINKED
- CONTACT # LINKED
- SECURITY QUESTION
- SECURITY ANSWER

NOTES

_____
_____
_____
_____
_____
_____
_____
_____
_____
_____

PASSWORD TRACKER

☐ SOC MEDIA   ☐ PERSONAL   ☐ WORK   ☐ GAMES   ☐ SHOPPING

- **WEBSITE**
- **USERNAME**
- **LOG IN/USER ID**
- **PASSWORD**
- **EMAIL LINKED**
- **CONTACT # LINKED**
- **SECURITY QUESTION**
- **SECURITY ANSWER**

NOTES

_____
_____
_____
_____
_____
_____
_____
_____
_____

PASSWORD TRACKER

| SOC MEDIA | PERSONAL | WORK | GAMES | SHOPPING |

- WEBSITE
- USERNAME
- LOG IN/USER ID
- PASSWORD
- EMAIL LINKED
- CONTACT # LINKED
- SECURITY QUESTION
- SECURITY ANSWER

NOTES
_____
_____
_____
_____
_____
_____
_____
_____
_____
_____

PASSWORD TRACKER

| ☐ SOC MEDIA | ☐ PERSONAL | ☐ WORK | ☐ GAMES | ☐ SHOPPING |

WEBSITE _____

USERNAME _____

LOG IN/USER ID _____

PASSWORD _____

EMAIL LINKED _____

CONTACT # LINKED _____

SECURITY QUESTION _____

SECURITY ANSWER _____

NOTES
_____
_____
_____
_____
_____
_____
_____
_____
_____
_____

PASSWORD TRACKER

| SOC MEDIA | PERSONAL | WORK | GAMES | SHOPPING |

- WEBSITE
- USERNAME
- LOG IN/USER ID
- PASSWORD
- EMAIL LINKED
- CONTACT # LINKED
- SECURITY QUESTION
- SECURITY ANSWER

NOTES

PASSWORD TRACKER

| SOC MEDIA | PERSONAL | WORK | GAMES | SHOPPING |

WEBSITE

USERNAME

LOG IN/USER ID

PASSWORD

EMAIL LINKED

CONTACT # LINKED

SECURITY QUESTION

SECURITY ANSWER

NOTES

PASSWORD TRACKER

| SOC MEDIA | PERSONAL | WORK | GAMES | SHOPPING |

- **WEBSITE**
- **USERNAME**
- **LOG IN/USER ID**
- **PASSWORD**
- **EMAIL LINKED**
- **CONTACT # LINKED**
- **SECURITY QUESTION**
- **SECURITY ANSWER**

NOTES

_____
_____
_____
_____
_____
_____
_____
_____
_____

PASSWORD TRACKER

| SOC MEDIA | PERSONAL | WORK | GAMES | SHOPPING |

WEBSITE

USERNAME

LOG IN/USER ID

PASSWORD

EMAIL LINKED

CONTACT # LINKED

SECURITY QUESTION

SECURITY ANSWER

NOTES

_____
_____
_____
_____
_____
_____
_____
_____
_____

PASSWORD TRACKER

☐ SOC MEDIA   ☐ PERSONAL   ☐ WORK   ☐ GAMES   ☐ SHOPPING

WEBSITE _____

USERNAME _____

LOG IN/USER ID _____

PASSWORD _____

EMAIL LINKED _____

CONTACT # LINKED _____

SECURITY QUESTION _____

SECURITY ANSWER _____

NOTES

_____
_____
_____
_____
_____
_____
_____
_____
_____

PASSWORD TRACKER

| ☐ SOC MEDIA | ☐ PERSONAL | ☐ WORK | ☐ GAMES | ☐ SHOPPING |

WEBSITE _____

USERNAME _____

LOG IN/USER ID _____

PASSWORD _____

EMAIL LINKED _____

CONTACT # LINKED _____

SECURITY QUESTION _____

SECURITY ANSWER _____

NOTES

_____
_____
_____
_____
_____
_____
_____
_____
_____

PASSWORD TRACKER

| SOC MEDIA | PERSONAL | WORK | GAMES | SHOPPING |

- WEBSITE
- USERNAME
- LOG IN/USER ID
- PASSWORD
- EMAIL LINKED
- CONTACT # LINKED
- SECURITY QUESTION
- SECURITY ANSWER

NOTES

PASSWORD TRACKER

| SOC MEDIA | PERSONAL | WORK | GAMES | SHOPPING |

WEBSITE

USERNAME

LOG IN/USER ID

PASSWORD

EMAIL LINKED

CONTACT # LINKED

SECURITY QUESTION

SECURITY ANSWER

NOTES

PASSWORD TRACKER

☐ SOC MEDIA ☐ PERSONAL ☐ WORK ☐ GAMES ☐ SHOPPING

- WEBSITE
- USERNAME
- LOG IN/USER ID
- PASSWORD
- EMAIL LINKED
- CONTACT # LINKED
- SECURITY QUESTION
- SECURITY ANSWER

NOTES

_____
_____
_____
_____
_____
_____
_____
_____
_____

PASSWORD TRACKER

☐ SOC MEDIA ☐ PERSONAL ☐ WORK ☐ GAMES ☐ SHOPPING

WEBSITE

USERNAME

LOG IN/USER ID

PASSWORD

EMAIL LINKED

CONTACT # LINKED

SECURITY QUESTION

SECURITY ANSWER

NOTES

_____
_____
_____
_____
_____
_____
_____
_____
_____

PASSWORD TRACKER

| SOC MEDIA | PERSONAL | WORK | GAMES | SHOPPING |

WEBSITE

USERNAME

LOG IN/USER ID

PASSWORD

EMAIL LINKED

CONTACT # LINKED

SECURITY QUESTION

SECURITY ANSWER

NOTES

_____
_____
_____
_____
_____
_____
_____
_____

PASSWORD TRACKER

| SOC MEDIA | PERSONAL | WORK | GAMES | SHOPPING |

WEBSITE

USERNAME

LOG IN/USER ID

PASSWORD

EMAIL LINKED

CONTACT # LINKED

SECURITY QUESTION

SECURITY ANSWER

NOTES

_____
_____
_____
_____
_____
_____
_____
_____
_____
_____

PASSWORD TRACKER

☐ SOC MEDIA ☐ PERSONAL ☐ WORK ☐ GAMES ☐ SHOPPING

WEBSITE _____

USERNAME _____

LOG IN/USER ID _____

PASSWORD _____

EMAIL LINKED _____

CONTACT # LINKED _____

SECURITY QUESTION _____

SECURITY ANSWER _____

NOTES

_____
_____
_____
_____
_____
_____
_____
_____
_____
_____

PASSWORD TRACKER

☐ SOC MEDIA   ☐ PERSONAL   ☐ WORK   ☐ GAMES   ☐ SHOPPING

WEBSITE

USERNAME

LOG IN/USER ID

PASSWORD

EMAIL LINKED

CONTACT # LINKED

SECURITY QUESTION

SECURITY ANSWER

NOTES

_____
_____
_____
_____
_____
_____
_____
_____
_____
_____

PASSWORD TRACKER

| SOC MEDIA | PERSONAL | WORK | GAMES | SHOPPING |

- WEBSITE
- USERNAME
- LOG IN/USER ID
- PASSWORD
- EMAIL LINKED
- CONTACT # LINKED
- SECURITY QUESTION
- SECURITY ANSWER

NOTES

_____
_____
_____
_____
_____
_____
_____
_____
_____

PASSWORD TRACKER

| SOC MEDIA | PERSONAL | WORK | GAMES | SHOPPING |

- **WEBSITE**
- **USERNAME**
- **LOG IN/USER ID**
- **PASSWORD**
- **EMAIL LINKED**
- **CONTACT # LINKED**
- **SECURITY QUESTION**
- **SECURITY ANSWER**

NOTES

_____
_____
_____
_____
_____
_____
_____
_____
_____

PASSWORD TRACKER

| SOC MEDIA | PERSONAL | WORK | GAMES | SHOPPING |

WEBSITE

USERNAME

LOG IN/USER ID

PASSWORD

EMAIL LINKED

CONTACT # LINKED

SECURITY QUESTION

SECURITY ANSWER

NOTES

_____
_____
_____
_____
_____
_____
_____
_____
_____
_____

PASSWORD TRACKER

☐ SOC MEDIA ☐ PERSONAL ☐ WORK ☐ GAMES ☐ SHOPPING

WEBSITE _____

USERNAME _____

LOG IN/USER ID _____

PASSWORD _____

EMAIL LINKED _____

CONTACT # LINKED _____

SECURITY QUESTION _____

SECURITY ANSWER _____

NOTES

_____
_____
_____
_____
_____
_____
_____
_____
_____
_____

PASSWORD TRACKER

| ☐ SOC MEDIA | ☐ PERSONAL | ☐ WORK | ☐ GAMES | ☐ SHOPPING |

WEBSITE

USERNAME

LOG IN/USER ID

PASSWORD

EMAIL LINKED

CONTACT # LINKED

SECURITY QUESTION

SECURITY ANSWER

NOTES

PASSWORD TRACKER

☐ SOC MEDIA   ☐ PERSONAL   ☐ WORK   ☐ GAMES   ☐ SHOPPING

WEBSITE

USERNAME

LOG IN/USER ID

PASSWORD

EMAIL LINKED

CONTACT # LINKED

SECURITY QUESTION

SECURITY ANSWER

NOTES

_____
_____
_____
_____
_____
_____
_____
_____
_____
_____

PASSWORD TRACKER

| SOC MEDIA | PERSONAL | WORK | GAMES | SHOPPING |

- WEBSITE
- USERNAME
- LOG IN/USER ID
- PASSWORD
- EMAIL LINKED
- CONTACT # LINKED
- SECURITY QUESTION
- SECURITY ANSWER

NOTES

PASSWORD TRACKER

☐ SOC MEDIA ☐ PERSONAL ☐ WORK ☐ GAMES ☐ SHOPPING

WEBSITE _____

USERNAME _____

LOG IN/USER ID _____

PASSWORD _____

EMAIL LINKED _____

CONTACT # LINKED _____

SECURITY QUESTION _____

SECURITY ANSWER _____

NOTES

_____
_____
_____
_____
_____
_____
_____
_____
_____
_____

PASSWORD TRACKER

☐ SOC MEDIA ☐ PERSONAL ☐ WORK ☐ GAMES ☐ SHOPPING

WEBSITE

USERNAME

LOG IN/USER ID

PASSWORD

EMAIL LINKED

CONTACT # LINKED

SECURITY QUESTION

SECURITY ANSWER

NOTES

_____
_____
_____
_____
_____
_____
_____
_____
_____
_____

PASSWORD TRACKER

☐ SOC MEDIA ☐ PERSONAL ☐ WORK ☐ GAMES ☐ SHOPPING

WEBSITE

USERNAME

LOG IN/USER ID

PASSWORD

EMAIL LINKED

CONTACT # LINKED

SECURITY QUESTION

SECURITY ANSWER

NOTES

_____
_____
_____
_____
_____
_____
_____
_____
_____
_____

PASSWORD TRACKER

| SOC MEDIA | PERSONAL | WORK | GAMES | SHOPPING |

- **WEBSITE**
- **USERNAME**
- **LOG IN/USER ID**
- **PASSWORD**
- **EMAIL LINKED**
- **CONTACT # LINKED**
- **SECURITY QUESTION**
- **SECURITY ANSWER**

NOTES

_____
_____
_____
_____
_____
_____
_____
_____
_____
_____

PASSWORD TRACKER

☐ SOC MEDIA ☐ PERSONAL ☐ WORK ☐ GAMES ☐ SHOPPING

WEBSITE

USERNAME

LOG IN/USER ID

PASSWORD

EMAIL LINKED

CONTACT # LINKED

SECURITY QUESTION

SECURITY ANSWER

NOTES

_____
_____
_____
_____
_____
_____
_____
_____
_____
_____

PASSWORD TRACKER

☐ SOC MEDIA   ☐ PERSONAL   ☐ WORK   ☐ GAMES   ☐ SHOPPING

WEBSITE

USERNAME

LOG IN/USER ID

PASSWORD

EMAIL LINKED

CONTACT # LINKED

SECURITY QUESTION

SECURITY ANSWER

NOTES

_____
_____
_____
_____
_____
_____
_____
_____
_____
_____

PASSWORD TRACKER

☐ SOC MEDIA ☐ PERSONAL ☐ WORK ☐ GAMES ☐ SHOPPING

WEBSITE

USERNAME

LOG IN/USER ID

PASSWORD

EMAIL LINKED

CONTACT # LINKED

SECURITY QUESTION

SECURITY ANSWER

NOTES

_____
_____
_____
_____
_____
_____
_____
_____
_____
_____

PASSWORD TRACKER

| SOC MEDIA | PERSONAL | WORK | GAMES | SHOPPING |

- WEBSITE
- USERNAME
- LOG IN/USER ID
- PASSWORD
- EMAIL LINKED
- CONTACT # LINKED
- SECURITY QUESTION
- SECURITY ANSWER

NOTES

_____
_____
_____
_____
_____
_____
_____
_____
_____
_____

PASSWORD TRACKER

☐ SOC MEDIA   ☐ PERSONAL   ☐ WORK   ☐ GAMES   ☐ SHOPPING

WEBSITE

USERNAME

LOG IN/USER ID

PASSWORD

EMAIL LINKED

CONTACT # LINKED

SECURITY QUESTION

SECURITY ANSWER

NOTES

_____
_____
_____
_____
_____
_____
_____
_____

PASSWORD TRACKER

| SOC MEDIA | PERSONAL | WORK | GAMES | SHOPPING |

- WEBSITE
- USERNAME
- LOG IN/USER ID
- PASSWORD
- EMAIL LINKED
- CONTACT # LINKED
- SECURITY QUESTION
- SECURITY ANSWER

NOTES

_____
_____
_____
_____
_____
_____
_____
_____
_____
_____

PASSWORD TRACKER

☐ SOC MEDIA ☐ PERSONAL ☐ WORK ☐ GAMES ☐ SHOPPING

WEBSITE

USERNAME

LOG IN/USER ID

PASSWORD

EMAIL LINKED

CONTACT # LINKED

SECURITY QUESTION

SECURITY ANSWER

NOTES

PASSWORD TRACKER

| SOC MEDIA | PERSONAL | WORK | GAMES | SHOPPING |

- WEBSITE
- USERNAME
- LOG IN/USER ID
- PASSWORD
- EMAIL LINKED
- CONTACT # LINKED
- SECURITY QUESTION
- SECURITY ANSWER

NOTES

PASSWORD TRACKER

| SOC MEDIA | PERSONAL | WORK | GAMES | SHOPPING |

WEBSITE

USERNAME

LOG IN/USER ID

PASSWORD

EMAIL LINKED

CONTACT # LINKED

SECURITY QUESTION

SECURITY ANSWER

NOTES

PASSWORD TRACKER

☐ SOC MEDIA ☐ PERSONAL ☐ WORK ☐ GAMES ☐ SHOPPING

- WEBSITE
- USERNAME
- LOG IN/USER ID
- PASSWORD
- EMAIL LINKED
- CONTACT # LINKED
- SECURITY QUESTION
- SECURITY ANSWER

NOTES

_____
_____
_____
_____
_____
_____
_____
_____
_____
_____

PASSWORD TRACKER

| SOC MEDIA | PERSONAL | WORK | GAMES | SHOPPING |

WEBSITE

USERNAME

LOG IN/USER ID

PASSWORD

EMAIL LINKED

CONTACT # LINKED

SECURITY QUESTION

SECURITY ANSWER

NOTES

_____
_____
_____
_____
_____
_____
_____
_____
_____
_____

PASSWORD TRACKER

| SOC MEDIA | PERSONAL | WORK | GAMES | SHOPPING |

- **WEBSITE**
- **USERNAME**
- **LOG IN/USER ID**
- **PASSWORD**
- **EMAIL LINKED**
- **CONTACT # LINKED**
- **SECURITY QUESTION**
- **SECURITY ANSWER**

NOTES

_____
_____
_____
_____
_____
_____
_____
_____
_____
_____